Fun in Autumn

Practicing the AU Sound

Amber King

Rosen
PHONICS
READERS

Rosen
Classroom™

August is over.
It is autumn!

Soon the leaves will fall.
Leaves fall fast!

Autumn is the best time of all.

Birds call to each other.
They fly south in autumn.

I watch football in autumn.
I love football!

My brother Paul and I
play ball, too.

I go to a haunted house.

The haunted house is tall.

We rake in autumn.
We make a small pile.

We fall into the leaves.

Do you call it autumn or fall?